Athena   Fall 2
              Monday

Misconceptions:
Morning Prayer — Be FULL of Thankfulness

ephesians

A **SIMPLY BIBLE** STUDY

CARMEN BEASLEY

To Jesus Christ, our humble Savior.

And to every woman seeking to
walk worthy of her calling...

Walk in a manner worthy of the calling
to which you have been called...

EPHESIANS 4:1

BY GRACE YOU

HAVE BEEN SAVED...

EPHESIANS 2:5

table of *contents*

EPHESIANS | A **SIMPLY BIBLE** STUDY

BUT GRACE WAS GIVEN
TO EACH ONE OF US
ACCORDING TO THE
MEASURE OF CHRIST'S GIFT.

EPHESIANS 4:7

welcome!

SHARING GOD'S STORY OF **SIMPLY BIBLE**

AS A LITTLE GIRL, I ADORED COLORING BOOKS. Smooth, crisp, white pages displayed bold black lines of perfectly-drawn figures and characters. The spaces patiently awaited color. Fondly, I remember the joy of opening a new pack of crayons. The neat little rows of pointed tips colorfully peeked out and tantalized me as if to say, "Try to choose just one!" Creativity awaited. Or so I thought.

When my four children were small, through a friend of a friend, I was encouraged to forgo coloring books. My initial reaction was one of horror. "What? Coloring books are fun! That would be forgoing fun! Plain paper? How boring!" Okay, granted… my reaction was a little melodramatic, but I do remember thinking these thoughts.

Instead, this friend insisted that providing children with blank sheets of paper was the way to spur creativity. I could see the wisdom. Not to mention, a ream of paper was way cheaper than four new coloring books… and so, I gave it a try. For the most part, my children simply grew up with lots of plain white paper and a variety of colorful pencils, crayons, and markers.

SIMPLE TOOLS LED TO ARTISTRY. My kids learned to draw. Not just little stick figures in the middle of the page, but they learned to tell a story using a piece of paper. Masterpieces. (At least in my eyes!)

Now I'm sure no one ever saved one of my coloring book pages. Oh, for sure! Sometimes one landed on Grandma's refrigerator. However, right now, down in my basement, binders of pictures remain—pictures that my budding artists created more than twenty years ago. Why? These pictures were windows into their little hearts and minds. These illustrations tell stories. And this mom treasures them in her heart.

THIS IS THE GIST OF **SIMPLY BIBLE**. My heart desires to provide women with a "blank page" for reading and engaging with God and His Word. Rather than fill-in-the-blank questions, this study offers space to observe, understand, and apply. Don't get me wrong: just like coloring books, traditional Bible studies have their place. I wouldn't be the Bible student that I am today without them. And yet, I am rather fond of this series. Basic tools and gentle direction allow for a quiet place where women are able to engage their hearts, souls, and minds with the intention of listening to and knowing God. It's a place for women to relate and retreat with Him by sharing in His story—simply the Bible.

TO BE HONEST, **SIMPLY BIBLE** ALMOST DIDN'T HAPPEN. Yep! I've shared this story before, but here it goes again. It's sort of embarrassing.

After much prayer as a newly-appointed women's ministry director of my church, I was assessing the state of our women's ministries when God pointed me toward inductive Bible study. Inductive study implies investigating the Bible directly. That's it. And so, in my mind, the conversation looked like this:

> **Me:** "Lord, You mean no video teaching and no fill-in-the-blank workbooks?
>
> **God:** "Yes. Take women directly to my Word."
>
> **Me:** "Lord, women like to have a book in their hands, and preferably one from a well-known author."
>
> **God:** "Use my Book."

So then, I obeyed. Ugh! I wish had immediately obeyed. Instead, and this is the embarrassing part, I played Gideon. I set my fleece out for God to prove His point, and I did it more than once. (If at this point you're doubting the validity of an author and a women's ministry leader who plays Gideon, I understand. You are welcome to return this book, no questions asked!) Instead of obeying, I purchased and reviewed every single Bible study available, at that time, on the gospel of John. Almost desperately, I was searching for something—anything—that would quietly and inductively walk women through that Gospel. One by one, God said "no." (Okay, it's not like God audibly spoke to me. But His Spirit has a way of getting His message across. You know what I mean?)

I continued to cry out to Him for a tool. Frankly, for years, as an experienced leader and Bible teacher, I had searched for a simple tool that does not require in-depth or extra training in order to teach or study inductively. I could not find one.

One day, while wrestling and praying over all of this, I sat down at my computer, opened a blank document, and began experimenting with the process of inductive study. I left my computer and went down to fix dinner. When I returned, I looked at what was on the paper and thought, "This works." Praise God! In perfect timing, He granted peace and direction.

He also led the way to Melissa Trew, a talented designer with a huge heart for God and His Word. She's a gift. Deftly, she takes this material, uses her God-giftedness, and turns it into something beautiful. Coffee-table worthy. Her designs are beyond anything I could begin to think or imagine. I'm grateful.

FINALLY, WHY INDUCTIVE STUDY? There are three main reasons, based on what today's woman says about Bible study:

FIRST: *"I feel inept. I know I should read the Bible. I want to, but I don't understand it."* Many women feel the same. With an influx of Bible study resources, we have relied on videos and books that give us the author's answers. It's easy to think we need an "expert" to intercede and interpret God's Word on our behalf. No doubt, there is a place for these resources, but we aren't to be dependent on them. We depend on God alone.

An old Chinese Proverb aptly says:

> Give a man a fish and you feed him for a day.
> Teach a man to fish and you feed him for a lifetime.

SIMPLY BIBLE is designed to equip women to "fish." By following the step-by-step framework, you can confidently approach God's Word. The inductive process of this journal eliminates my voice as much as possible, with the hopes that you can listen to God's voice alone. That's the beauty of inductive study: rather than listening to *an* author, we listen directly to *the* Author. My prayer is that, through His Word, we will experience the incredible joy and adventure of personal encounters with Him. And then? We share Him with others.

SECOND: *"I'm busy. Overwhelmed by demands. Life is crazy!"*
I know. I feel it too. This study should maximize time. Rather than spending time reading other books, watching videos, filling in the blanks, and checking Bible study off our "to-do" list, we skip the "middle-man" and go directly to God and His Word. Immediately, we relate with Him one-on-one.

Truly, this study can be catered to the needs of the busy woman who can barely scrape together ten minutes a day for Bible study. Yet, it can also fit the need of the woman who longs to linger and dig deeper into the Word. Kind of like scuba diving, you'll choose how deep you want to go and how far you'd like to roam.

THIRD: *"I need relationship. Do others care about me?"*
Today's younger woman is seeking connection. Her desire? To be seen, known, and loved. Video teaching often does not meet her expressed need because it takes time away from deeper relationship-building—both with Christ and with others. Although she is hungry to know, the bottom line is that she prefers personal interaction. And the discussion had better be relevant and meaningful, with no pat answers.

Concurringly, a generation of women my age is now dependent on video teachers and fill-in-the-blank studies, rather than dependent on God and His Word. Because of her dependency on these tools, a veteran Bible student is often ill-equipped to read the Bible for herself and even more ill-equipped to share her faith and God's Word with others.

Inductive study maximizes time and develops skills to focus on real relationship and interaction with God and others. Why **SIMPLY BIBLE**? To focus on the "relationship need" now felt acutely within women's ministries across the country.

CONSIDER FAST FOOD VERSUS A HOME-COOKED MEAL. Picking up fast food can be a treat. It's quick and easy. It's downright helpful to have someone else prepare and hand you the meal. Much of our Bible study resources are similar to "fast food." Someone else does the preparation and serves up a quick and easy word of encouragement. It's helpful, but it's not "home-cooked." Rarely would we serve fast food to friends or carry it to a potluck. The same holds true for feasting on God's Word. Inductive study allows for that special and intimate meal meant to be shared with others.

SO THAT'S A GOD-AT-WORK STORY. That's how **SIMPLY BIBLE** was birthed.

Since its inception, I've had the joy and privilege of watching women journal and seek God through these study workbooks. These journals are windows into hearts, souls, and minds growing with God. These notebooks tell stories. And although they are much too private for me to observe closely, I treasure them in my heart. If I could, I'd pile them up in my basement.

For each woman who has braved a **SIMPLY BIBLE** study, I am truly grateful. In a sense, there is a basement in my heart where memories of studying with you are tucked away. Thank you. You spur me on to dig deep into God's Word, to know and love Him and others more deeply.

If you are new, you've probably gathered by now that this study is different. And different often falls outside our comfort zones. The purpose of this journal is that you may confidently read, understand, and apply God's Word like you've never before experienced, using *simply* the Bible. It will require a commitment.

COMMIT. There's no "Oh, I'll just give it a try." Commit to see this study through to the finish.

If the inductive Bible study process is new to you, don't be intimidated. My first home-cooked meal didn't look or taste anything like my mom's meal. Cooking takes practice. Even after forty some years of cooking, most of what I cook tastes different from my mom's cooking. The same will be true for Bible study. Inductive study will take practice. Your study will look different from most others. You are unique and special. And so, your study insights and application will be unique. But, by the end, you will better know Jesus Christ, His Word, and your identity in Him. You are loved, valued, and treasured by an amazing God.

SO WELCOME TO **SIMPLY BIBLE**! And welcome to this particular series of Galatians, Ephesians, Philippians, and Colossians.

These epistles (or letters), written by the Apostle Paul, share a window into a heart set free to fully know and seek God. As we engage and share in God's Word, like Paul, may we yield our hearts and minds to God's heart, having the mind of Christ Jesus. And may He permeate and etch His fruit of love, joy, peace, patience, kindness, goodness, faithfulness, gentleness, and self-control onto the pages of our own hearts, for His glory.

I'm praying for you and with you.

With much love and joy,

Carmen

getting *started*

A QUICK-START GUIDE TO **SIMPLY BIBLE**

IN HIM WE HAVE
REDEMPTION THROUGH
HIS BLOOD...

EPHESIANS 1:7

getting *started*
AN INTRODUCTION TO INDUCTIVE BIBLE STUDY

Recently, a friend described **SIMPLY BIBLE** as "leaving behind her paint-by-numbers set for a blank canvas." Of course, her word picture melted my heart! But honestly, whether painting or digging into God's Word, using a blank canvas can be a little intimidating. It takes practice! Just as an artist learns a particular method and handles special tools to create a masterpiece, so do Bible study students.

The inductive Bible study method involves three basic steps that often overlap:
- **(1)** Observe
- **(2)** Interpret
- **(3)** Apply

Using the **SIMPLY BIBLE** format will help to paint a more thorough understanding of God's Word.

On the following pages, you will find a quick-start guide to **SIMPLY BIBLE**. This guide is followed by a more thorough explanation of the format and basic study tools. Take time to get a feel for them.

And then... dig in!

a quick start to *simply bible*

A STEP-BY-STEP GUIDE

READ	OBSERVE	INTERPRET
Read the passage. Try some of the following ideas to help you read carefully. (Highlighters and colored pencils are fun here!)	As you read, write down your observations in this column. Simply notice what the Scripture *says*. This is your place for notes. Ideas include:	In this column, record what the passage *means*.
• Read the passage in a different version.	• Ask questions of the text, like "who, what, when, where, or how."	One way to interpret is to answer any questions asked during observation. Try to first answer these *without* the aid of other helps. Allow Scripture to explain Scripture. It often does.
• Read it out loud.	• Jot down key items: people, places, things. Mark places on a map.	If the answers are not intuitive or easily found near the passage, other tools are available. Use boxes A, B, and C to identify a key word, define it, and look up a cross reference. This extra research will shed light on the meaning.
• Underline, circle, box, or highlight repeated words, unfamiliar words, or anything that catches your attention.	• Ask, "What does this Scripture passage say about Jesus?"	
• Listen to the passage while running errands.	• Note what took place before and after this passage.	IMPORTANT: Seek to understand what the passage meant to the author and his original readers. Try to look at the world through the eyes of early Christians.
• Doodle or write out a verse in a journaling Bible.	• Ponder.	
	• Ask God if there is anything else He'd like you to notice.	

PLEASE NOTE: The following boxes (labeled A, B, and C) are interpretation tools. These are meant to be used in unison with the "Interpret" column on the previous page to aid in interpreting Scripture. Most women find it helpful to complete these *before* interpreting. Find what's most helpful for you.

A KEY WORDS	**B** DEFINITIONS	**C** CROSS REFERENCES
When you notice a word that is repeated multiple times, is unfamiliar, or is interesting to you in any other way, record it here.	Here, record definitions of your key words. You can find the appropriate definitions by using: • a Bible concordance (defines words according to the original language) • a Bible dictionary • another translation	Note cross references. This is a solid way to allow Scripture to interpret Scripture. If your Bible does not include cross references, they can be found easily using web-based Bible resources.

Bible study tools like those listed above can be found by visiting the following websites:

blueletterbible.org   **biblegateway.com**   **biblehub.com**

MAIN POINTS	APPLY
Summarize the main point(s) or note any themes you encountered in the passage.	Apply God's Word specifically to your own life. Application is personal. God may teach, correct, rebuke, or train. He is always equipping. (II Tim. 3:16-17) Record what this passage means to you.

PRAY

Write a short prayer here. When we take time to write something down, that message becomes more etched on our heart. Take a moment to simply be with God. He is why we study. Savor. Know. Praise. Confess. Thank. Ask. Love. Then carry a nugget of His Word in your heart to ponder and proclaim throughout your day.

BUT GOD, BEING RICH
IN MERCY... MADE US
ALIVE TOGETHER
WITH CHRIST...

EPHESIANS 2:4-5

step by *step*

UNPACKING THE INDUCTIVE METHOD

step by *step*

UNPACKING THE INDUCTIVE METHOD

STEPS 1 & 2: READ AND OBSERVE | *See what the Bible **says**.*
The first step to Bible study is simply reading God's Word.

The problem is that, in our hurried, scurried pace of life, we often plow right through it without taking time to ponder and think about what we're reading. *Observing* what we read helps us to slow down and take notice in order to see and answer, "What does the Bible *say*?"

Have you ever slowed down to truly examine and enjoy a piece of art? Artists have an amazing knack or ability to capture a particular scene, whether real or imagined, onto a blank canvas. How? Artists specialize in observing details. Setting, color, texture, time, characters, lighting, movement... the list of details is nearly limitless.

We can do this, too.

When they were young, blank sketch pads and new drawing pencils became a special treat for my children. Now imagine me with my small army of little ones traipsing off to a park with these tools in hand. Before pulling out a pencil to begin creating, the first thing to do was to find the right spot. (I highly recommend that for Bible study, too!) Then we'd observe.

To observe means "to see, watch, notice, or regard with attention, especially so as to see or learn something."[1] *Especially so as to see or learn something.*

And so, with my children, we would notice things. Lots of things! The different types of leaves, flowers, plants, grass, insects, animals, and more. Once engaged in observing, details begin to arise! How fun to zero in and observe the lady bug crawling along the

---

[1] **ethos**. Dictionary.com. *Dictionary.com Unabridged*. Random House, Inc. http://www.dictionary.com/browse/ethos (accessed: March 16, 2018).

blade of grass or the spots that adorn a toad sunning on the sidewalk or the veins that run throughout a maple leaf. There's so much to see!

Observation implies being curious. Noticing details. Asking questions.

Kids do this naturally. We can too. Be curious with God's Word. Scripture is full of details to notice and so many questions to ask. When we slow down to "smell the roses" within Scripture, we will see and learn something.

As you read, ask God's help to see what He would have you to see. Ask questions of the text and highlight verses that touch your heart. If anything is especially noteworthy to you, jot it down in the space to observe. (Keep in mind: this framework is simply a guide. You can fill in as little or as much of the space as you desire.)

The bottom line? Read. Read carefully. Then observe at least one thing. By doing so, we will see Scripture more clearly.

STEP 3: INTERPRET | *Understand what the Bible* **means**.

After careful observation of a landscape, an artist sketches an *interpretation* of what he sees onto the canvas. Observation and interpretation go hand in hand. A circle is a circle. A square is a square. As closely as possible, the artist defines and places an image of what he observes onto the canvas. Careful observation leads to a life-like rendering such that the viewer will enjoy a solid understanding of what the artist himself observed.

The same is true of the Bible. Observation and interpretation go hand in hand. Scripture will often interpret Scripture. As we carefully read and observe what the scripture says, we frequently understand and simultaneously interpret it's meaning. So, within our daily study format, observation and interpretation are located side-by-side.

One simple way to understand the meaning of Scripture is to answer any questions that we've asked of the text. Try answering them without the aid of study notes or other helps. Utilize scripture to interpret scripture.

Other times, interpretation is not so easy. After all, the Bible was written in ancient times, spanning the course of over 2,000 years, by a people and to a people of a culture that is utterly foreign to us.

Therefore, certain resources are handy. These tools help us to place and understand Scripture in its original context, in order to properly interpret what we've read. (Think of an artist pulling out a ruler—a simple tool that helps to more accurately reproduce a scene. A ruler is not necessary, but is useful.)

Bible study tools can include:

- *Cross references:* Cross references allow us to use nearby or related passages to more accurately interpret Scripture.
- *Bible dictionaries and concordances:* These tools allow us to understand the meaning of a word in its original language.
- *Bible handbooks and commentaries:* Resources like these help us to verify our conclusions as well as provide historical or cultural context.

It's important to remember that Scripture, in its original context, had only one meaning. Not multiple meanings. And although God can be mysterious, there are no mystical or hidden meanings within Scripture. Paul had a specific message, written at a specific time and in a specific place, for a specific group of people. He meant what he said. For this study, we want to know what Paul *meant* and how his audience *understood* him. Although we may not always be able to determine Paul's specific intent, that is our goal.

Interpretation implies understanding. Original meaning and context are important. Be reasonable. Compare.

Seek correct answers, but give yourself grace. A child's rendering of a ladybug on a blade of grass will not compare to Van Gogh's renderings, and yet, there is something wholly precious about the works of a child. Our renderings of Scripture won't ever equate to a Bible scholar's commentary. That's not our goal here. Our goal is knowing God. Sometimes this involves baby steps.

A, B, & C: TOOLS FOR INTERPRETATION

If the answers are not intuitive or easily found within the passage, tools are available to help us better understand. Our daily lesson format provides three boxes intended to support interpretation. Here, you'll find space to identify key words, define those key words, and record supporting vereses (cross references). These are intended to help and guide you as you interpret Scripture. Use them however you find them to be helpful.

A. KEY WORDS: Did you notice that a word was repeated, seems important, is unfamiliar, or is interesting in any way? Record it here.

B. DEFINITIONS: Use this box to record definitions of the key words you listed. For definitions, we have options:

• *Read the verse using a different translation or version of the Bible.* This can be a very simple way to define a word. For example, our practice lesson (on page 22) notes the word **apostle** from I Timothy 1:1. The ESV translation says "apostle," while the Amplified Bible expounds: "apostle (special messenger, personally chosen representative)." [1]

• *Use a Bible concordance.* My favorite way to define a word is to use a concordance. This tool looks at words in their original language. I like the **Strong's Concordance**, which can also be found online.

i. Going online? Try **Blue Letter Bible**, a free web-based concordance.

ii. Once there, (referring to our practice lesson on page 22) simply type "I Timothy 1" into the "Search the Bible" box. Click on the box

---

[1] The Holy Bible: The Amplified Bible. 1987. La Habra, CA: The Lockman Foundation.

called **TOOLS** next to I Timothy 1:1 and an assortment of choices will arrive. Find the corresponding Strong's Concordance number for "apostle" (in this case: G652) and click on it. You'll retrieve the Greek word, original definitions, and how it is used in other places of the Bible. It's fascinating! Make note of the definitions you find.

• *Try a Bible dictionary.* In order to define people or find places, Bible dictionaries are handy.

i. Online, you can try **Bible Gateway, Blue Letter Bible,** or **Bible Hub** for free.

ii. There are also wonderful apps available for you to use. A friend recently introduced me to **Bible Map.** This app is simple to use and automatically syncs Scripture with maps.

C. CROSS REFERENCES: Some Bibles offer cross references. This is a solid way to allow Scripture to interpret Scripture. Perhaps your Bible does not include cross references (most journaling Bibles do not). No worries! It's very easy to access cross references online. **Bible Hub** is a great place to start!

Your daily lesson framework also offers space for you to identify the main point of the passage you've read. Here, you may summarize the main point(s) or any recurring themes you noticed in the passage. Understanding the main idea always helps us to interpret a scenario correctly.

WANTING EVEN MORE? Our daily study format includes space for key words, definitions, and cross references, along with space to identify the main points of the passage you're studying. However, there are other helps available if you'd like to dig deeper. Biblical commentaries are books written by Biblical scholars. Commentaries often provide solid cultural and historical context while commenting verse-by-verse on Scripture.

Personally, I admire the dedication and genius of the scholars who write commentaries. These amazingly dedicated scholars study for the glory of God. And yet, it's best to save these resources for last. Why? Because commentaries are not a substitute for reading and understanding God's Word on your own. Seek to understand on your own first.

Also, please note that commentaries are often written according to various theological bents. It's helpful to compare. Know your sources. This is especially crucial if roaming the Internet. Please surf with discernment and great care.

Still not satisfied? Note your question and talk to God about it. Ponder. Many times, as you ponder a verse, God will interpret. Other times, He allows certain things to remain a mystery. He is sovereign. We walk by faith.

Remember to share and discuss your questions with others at Bible study, either in person or online. Studying God's Word is meant to be done in community. We encourage, learn, and grow together.

Finally, check out our website: **www.simplybible.study**.

STEP 4: APPLICATION | *Put it all **together**.*

With the Holy Spirit's illumination, careful observation, and good interpretation, we better understand the meaning of a passage. And that's thrilling! Oftentimes, finding a nugget of truth, a promise, or a revelation about God Himself takes my breath away! There is no other book like it:

> For the word of God is living and active, sharper than any two-edged sword, piercing to the division of soul and of spirit, of joints and of marrow, and discerning the thoughts and intentions of the heart.
> *Hebrews 4:12*

The God of the Universe loves us and personally reveals Himself through His Living Word. When He does, it cuts in a good way. Then we're ready to *apply* His Word to our everyday lives.

Application is the fun and creative part. Yes, the original author of Scripture had one meaning, but the personal applications of Scripture are many. This part is between you and God. A particular verse, word, or idea might strike a chord in your heart. Slow down. Take note. Show God the discovery. This is the amazing process of God revealing Himself and His truth to you through His Word and the power of His Holy Spirit.

God looks at our hearts. He sees, knows, and loves His sheep. And so, He may use His Word to teach, correct, rebuke, or train. He is always equipping. (II Timothy 3:16-17) If you're willing, He will lead you to apply His Word specifically to your everyday life.

Application ideas include:
1. Worship God for who He is, according to a truth or promised discovered.
2. Thank Him for a lesson learned.
3. Note an example to follow.
4. Confess a sin revealed.
5. Pray a prayer noticed.
6. Obey, trust, and follow God's way, His command, His plan.
7. Memorize a verse.

WRAPPING UP: PRAYER | *Respond to a **holy** God.*

Application implies a recognition of who God is. And so, wrapping up personal study with application nearly always leads me to bow down in worship, at least bowing my heart. Hence, the **SIMPLY BIBLE** daily format includes a place for *prayer*. Please use this! It may be the most important space of all.

Enjoy being together with Him in His Word. Savor. Learn. Grow. Know. Thank. Praise. Love. Then carry a nugget of truth in your heart to ponder with Him as you go about your day.

lesson *samples*

PRACTICE LESSONS & EXAMPLES

practice *lesson*

A STEP-BY-STEP GUIDE

Below are two verses, I Timothy 1:1-2. As you read, feel free to highlight, circle, underline and mark up the text in whatever way you like. In the *Observe* column, jot down details that pop out and write down questions that come to mind. Then interpret. Simply use the Scripture itself or hop over to boxes A, B, and C to define a word or find a cross reference that will help you better understand.

Finish by summarizing, applying, and praying.

This is *your* workbook. It is meant to be a journal of your thoughts as you engage with God and His Word. Don't be shy. Be you, be with God, and enjoy!

READ	OBSERVE	INTERPRET
[1] Paul, an apostle of Christ Jesus by command of God our Savior and of Christ Jesus our hope, [2] To Timothy, my true child in the faith: Grace, mercy, and peace from God the Father and Christ Jesus our Lord.		

KEY WORDS	DEFINITIONS	CROSS REFERENCES

MAIN POINT(S)

APPLY

PRAY

sample *lesson*

1 TIMOTHY 1:1-2 | FOR THOSE CRAZY, BUSY DAYS

Life gets hectic. We get busy. It happens. Some days, you just don't have the time to go very deep in your study. That's okay! But even reading just a few verses and aiming to hone in on *one* important detail is better than nothing at all! Here's what it might look like to observe, interpret, and apply just *one* thing:

READ	OBSERVE	INTERPRET
¹ Paul, an apostle of Christ Jesus by command of God our Savior and of Christ Jesus our hope, ² To Timothy, my true child in the faith: Grace, mercy, and peace from God the Father and Christ Jesus our Lord.	Christ Jesus is mentioned 3 times. According to Paul, who is he?	Jesus is "our hope." He is "our Lord." He commanded Paul to be His apostle. He gives grace, mercy, and peace.

KEY WORDS	DEFINITIONS	CROSS REFERENCES
apostle	a special messenger, a personally-chosen representative (Amplified Bible)	**I Timothy 1:12** I thank him who has given me strength, Christ Jesus our Lord, because he judged me faithful, appointing me to his service...

MAIN POINT(S)

The apostle Paul greets Timothy in a letter.

APPLY

Even in a greeting of a letter, Paul brings glory to Jesus and reminds Timothy of the hope we have in Him. How can I greet others with this same exuberance for Christ throughout my day today?

PRAY

Lord God, thank You for today's reminder of hope. I praise You, Jesus, for **you are Lord.** And You are the giver of grace, mercy, and peace. Thank You! Like Paul, may I be a vessel of Your hope, grace, mercy, and peace today.

sample *lesson*

1 TIMOTHY 1:1-2 | GOING DEEPER

On occasion, you may find yourself wanting to go a little deeper in your study. Here's an example of what that could look like. You can observe as much or as little as you like. Remember: no two journals will look the same.

READ	OBSERVE	INTERPRET
[1] Paul, an apostle of Christ Jesus by command of God our Savior and of Christ Jesus our hope,	Who is Paul?	Paul: an apostle of Jesus.
	What is an apostle?	Apostle: chosen by God
[2] To Timothy, my true child in the faith:	Christ Jesus is mentioned 3 times in two verses! Who is He?	Jesus is our hope and our Lord. He commanded Paul to be His apostle. He gives grace, mercy, and peace.
Grace, mercy, and peace from God the Father and Christ Jesus our Lord.	Why is He our hope?	Christ is our Savior. He is also "in us." (Col.1:27)
	Who is Timothy?	
	Paul refers to Timothy as "my" true child. Why?	Timothy: Paul's "true child in the faith." Not sure why Paul uses this phrase. Perhaps Paul witnessed to Timothy and was a part of his spiritual "birth."
	Faith in what?	Faith: Belief in Christ.
	Is it common to offer grace, mercy, and peace in a greeting?	Mercy is found in other greetings: II Timothy 1, 2 John 3, Jude 2, but overall is unique for Paul to include in his letters.
	Notice Paul distinguishes between God the Father and Jesus Christ.	

KEY WORDS	DEFINITIONS	CROSS REFERENCES
apostle	a special messenger, a personally-chosen representative (Amplified Bible)	**I Timothy 1:12** - I thank him who has given me strength, Christ Jesus our Lord, because he judged me faithful, appointing me to his service...
hope	an expectation	**Colossians 1:27** - To them God chose to make known how great among the Gentiles are the riches of the glory of this mystery, which is Christ in you, the hope of glory.
true child in the faith		**Titus 1:4** - To Titus, my true child in a common faith...

MAIN POINT(S)

The apostle Paul greets Timothy in a letter.

APPLY

Even in a greeting, Paul brings glory to Jesus and reminds Timothy of the hope we have in Him. How can I greet others with this same exuberance for Christ? What am I doing to "give birth" to children of the faith? Praise God for His grace, peace, and mercy! Am I extending this to others?

PRAY

Lord God, thank You for today's reminder of hope. I praise You, Jesus, for **you are Lord.** And You are the giver of grace, mercy, and peace. Thank You! Like Paul, may I be a vessel of Your hope, grace, mercy, and peace today. Lord, I pray for open doors to share Christ with _____. Please prepare her heart to receive your grace and peace.

YOU DID IT! That's it. That's all there is to it. If this is your first time, perhaps the process felt awkward. Don't worry. You probably don't remember how clumsy and time-consuming it was the very first time you tried tying your shoe, riding a bike, or driving a car. Practice helps. Same for Bible study.

You're more observant, smarter, and stronger than you think you are. God created you that way. More importantly, He is with you. His desire is to be known. Lean into Him. Ask, seek, and you will find. His grace is sufficient. His power is made perfect in our weakness.

> For as the rain and the snow come down from heaven
>   and do not return there but water the earth,
> making it bring forth and sprout,
>   giving seed to the sower and bread to the eater,
> so shall my word be that goes out from my mouth;
>   it shall not return to me empty,
> but it shall accomplish that which I purpose,
>   and shall succeed in the thing for which I sent it.
> For you shall go out in joy
>   and be led forth in peace;
> the mountains and the hills before you
>   shall break forth into singing,
>   and all the trees of the field shall clap their hands.
>
> *Isaiah 55:10-12*

Lord God Almighty, thank You for Your Word! Like rain and snow watering the earth so that it might bud and flourish, may Your Word now water our hearts, minds, and souls to flourish in our love for You and for one another. May Your purposes and desires be accomplished. As we study with You, may we go out in joy and be led forth in Your peace. With all creation may we sing and clap for joy and bring glory to Your Name...

in *context*

EXAMINING THE CONTEXT OF EPHESIANS

in *context*

EPHESIANS: A letter written by the Apostle Paul to the Gentiles in Ephesus. Ephesus is the setting for Acts 19, where on his third mission trip in Asia, Paul spent two years teaching daily (Acts 19:9). We also know that the elders from Ephesus came to see Paul before his last journey to Jerusalem (Acts 20:17–18).

This bustling port city on the Aegean Sea was strategically located within Asia Minor and was a vital location for commerce, politics, and government. Not only this, but it was also strategically located for sharing the good news of Jesus Christ. In its heyday, Ephesus stood as home to the temple of Artemis, making it a religious center as well. People traveled great distances to see this wonder of the ancient world.

The style of Paul's letter to the Ephesians is unique. At times using liturgical and worshipful praise, Paul points to the majestic greatness and power of the Lord Jesus Christ, who unites both Jews and Gentiles in His church. Gracefully and poignantly intertwined within this epistle lies a beautiful theology for the church.

Here, Paul reminds believers of their identity "in Christ" and motivates them to "walk worthy" of their calling in daily living. His point? The spiritual walk of Christians ought to be grounded in their spiritual wealth. Themes of divine gifts—adoption, redemption, inheritance, power, life, grace, citizenship, and the love of Christ— abound in the first half of the letter. The second half is chock full of helpful guidelines for living out Christlikeness and concludes with Paul's final motivation to "armor up."

Encouraging and strengthening, the book of Ephesians will remind us that behavior does not determine blessing, but that our abundant blessings ought to determine our behavior. Let's join the Ephesians and learn to "walk worthy."

the roman *empire*

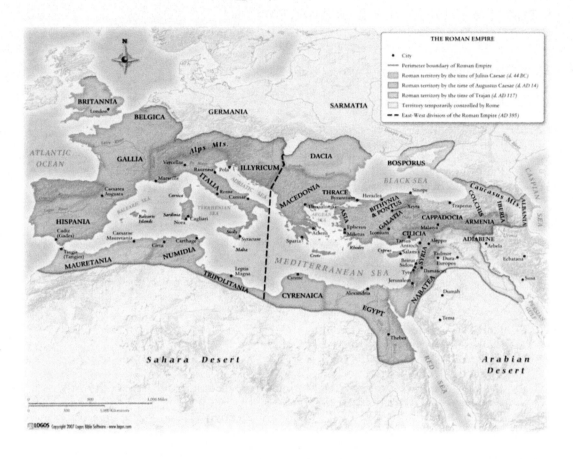

---

[1] Map provided by Logos Bible Software.

keeping *time*

A TIMELINE OF PAUL'S JOURNEY

28 — Jesus' public ministry begins (28-30)

30 — Jesus' crucifixion

32 —

Paul's conversion

34 —

Paul's first post-conversion Jerusalem visit

36 — Paul in Cilicia and Syria (35-46)

38 —

40 —

42 —

44 —

46 — Paul's second Jerusalem visit
Paul and Barnabus in Cyprus and Galatia

48 — *Paul writes his letter to the Galatians (?)*
Council of Jerusalem

50 — Paul & Silas travel from Syrian Antioch to Macedonia and Achaia (49-50)
Paul writes his letter to the Thessalonians

52 — Paul in Corinth (50-52); Paul's third Jerusalem visit
Paul in Ephesus (52-55)

54 —

Paul writes his letters to the Corinthians (55-56)

56 — Paul in Macedonia, Illyricum, and Achaia
Paul writes his letter to the Romans; Paul's final Jerusalem visit

58 — Paul's imprisonment in Caesarea (57-59)
Paul's voyage to Rome begins

60 — Paul arrives in Rome
Paul placed under house-arrest in Rome (60-62)

62 — *Paul writes his "captivity letters" (60-62?)*

64 —

---

[1] Bruce, F. F. (2000). *Paul, Apostle of the Heart Set Free*. Cumbria, UK: Paternoster Press.

32 ephesians • SIMPLY BIBLE

walking *worthy*

COUNT YOUR BLESSINGS

In Paul's letter to the Ephesians, he reminds us of our incredible riches in Christ. This collection of blessings belongs to all believers, but unfortunately, we don't always remember or acknowledge just how rich we are. We end up living as if we are spiritual "paupers." To help you stay mindful of your spiritual wealth, use this chart to keep an account of the blessings you see in your own life. For each blessing you note, give a brief description and a Scripture reference.

BLESSING	DESCRIPTION	REFERENCE
Son's Husband		

walking *worthy*

COUNT YOUR BLESSINGS

BLESSING	DESCRIPTION	REFERENCE

the armor of *god*

BECOMING A **DOER** OF THE WORD

the armor of God *challenge*

BECOMING A **DOER** OF THE WORD

In his letter to the Ephesians, Paul reminds us that our battle is a spiritual one. He exhorts us to be strong in the Lord and to "put on" the whole armor of God. Do you want to learn how to fight this battle while fully equipped? Complete the "armor of God challenge" during this **SIMPLY BIBLE** study and watch as God continues His good work in you!

Each week throughout our study, choose to focus on one piece of our "equipment." Begin by *defining* it. Then, find practical ways to ponder and practice *living* it. Record one thought or action each day related to wielding this piece of armor.

> Therefore take up the whole armor of God, that you may be able to withstand in the evil day, and having done all, to stand firm. Stand therefore, having fastened on the belt of truth, and having put on the breastplate of righteousness, and, as shoes for your feet, having put on the readiness given by the gospel of peace. In all circumstances take up the shield of faith, with which you can extinguish all the flaming darts of the evil one; and take the helmet of salvation, and the sword of the Spirit, which is the word of God, praying at all times in the Spirit, with all prayer and supplication.
> *Ephesians 6:13-18*

WEEK	THE BELT OF TRUTH — ① Ask Jesus to accept / be Savior — aknowledge
DEFINE	Gird up your loins
SUNDAY	The word of God can be found anywhere
MONDAY	Fellowship is a Blessing
TUESDAY	
WEDNESDAY	· ·· God is with me
THURSDAY	
FRIDAY	· · Joy at all times
SATURDAY	

WEEK	THE BREASTPLATE OF RIGHTEOUSNESS
DEFINE	
SUNDAY	
MONDAY	
TUESDAY	
WEDNESDAY	
THURSDAY	
FRIDAY	
SATURDAY	

WEEK	THE SHOES OF READINESS
DEFINE	

SUNDAY	
MONDAY	
TUESDAY	
WEDNESDAY	
THURSDAY	
FRIDAY	
SATURDAY	

WEEK	THE SHIELD OF FAITH
DEFINE	

SUNDAY	
MONDAY	
TUESDAY	
WEDNESDAY	
THURSDAY	
FRIDAY	
SATURDAY	

WEEK	THE HELMET OF SALVATION
DEFINE	

SUNDAY	
MONDAY	
TUESDAY	
WEDNESDAY	
THURSDAY	
FRIDAY	
SATURDAY	

WEEK	THE SWORD OF THE SPIRIT
DEFINE	

SUNDAY	
MONDAY	
TUESDAY	
WEDNESDAY	
THURSDAY	
FRIDAY	
SATURDAY	

FOR AT ONE TIME YOU
WERE DARKNESS, BUT
NOW YOU ARE LIGHT
IN THE LORD. WALK AS
CHILDREN OF LIGHT...

EPHESIANS 5:8

chapter *one*

EPHESIANS

take *note*

NOTES ON EPHESIANS 1

take *note*

NOTES ON EPHESIANS 1

day *one*

EPHESIANS 1:1-6

READ	OBSERVE	INTERPRET
[1] Paul, an apostle of Christ Jesus by the will of God, To the saints who are in Ephesus, and are faithful in Christ Jesus: [2] Grace to you and peace from God our Father and the Lord Jesus Christ. [3] Blessed be the God and Father of our Lord Jesus Christ, who has blessed us in Christ with every spiritual blessing in the heavenly places, [4] even as he chose us in him before the foundation of the world, that we should be holy and blameless before him. In love [5] he predestined us for adoption to himself as sons through Jesus Christ, according to the purpose of his will, [6] to the praise of his glorious grace, with which he has blessed us in the Beloved.	apostle	grace peace bless

KEY WORDS	DEFINITIONS	CROSS REFERENCES
saints	person that ~~when~~ is holy and will be in heaven after death.	
chose	set apart one of many	God chose ~~Israelites~~ John 10:16 sheep
apostle		

MAIN POINT(S)

Chosen

Blessed
Adoptiaon
His Will & Glory

APPLY

In Him
His Will His Glory
Predestined

PRAY

day *two*

EPHESIANS 1:7-12

READ	OBSERVE	INTERPRET
7 In him we have redemption through his blood, the forgiveness of our trespasses, according to the riches of his grace, 8 which he lavished upon us, in all wisdom and insight 9 making known to us the mystery of his will, according to his purpose, which he set forth in Christ 10 as a plan for the fullness of time, to unite all things in him, things in heaven and things on earth. 11 In him we have obtained an inheritance, having been predestined according to the purpose of him who works all things according to the counsel of his will, 12 so that we who were the first to hope in Christ might be to the praise of his glory.		

KEY WORDS	DEFINITIONS	CROSS REFERENCES

MAIN POINT(S)

APPLY

PRAY

day *three*

EPHESIANS 1:13-14

READ	OBSERVE	INTERPRET
[13] In him you also, when you heard the word of truth, the gospel of your salvation, and believed in him, were sealed with the promised Holy Spirit, [14] who is the guarantee of our inheritance until we acquire possession of it, to the praise of his glory.		

KEY WORDS	DEFINITIONS	CROSS REFERENCES

MAIN POINT(S)

APPLY

PRAY

day *four*

EPHESIANS 1:15-23

READ	OBSERVE	INTERPRET
[15] For this reason, because I have heard of your faith in the Lord Jesus and your love toward all the saints, [16] I do not cease to give thanks for you, remembering you in my prayers, [17] that the God of our Lord Jesus Christ, the Father of glory, may give you the Spirit of wisdom and of revelation in the knowledge of him, [18] having the eyes of your hearts enlightened, that you may know what is the hope to which he has called you, what are the riches of his glorious inheritance in the saints, [19] and what is the immeasurable greatness of his power toward us who believe, according to the working of his great might [20] that he worked in Christ when he raised him from the dead and seated him at his right hand in the heavenly places, [21] far above all rule and authority and power and dominion, and above every name that is named, not only in this age but also in the one to come. [22] And he put all things under his feet and gave him as head over all things to the church, [23] which is his body, the fullness of him who fills all in all.		

ps 46:10 - Be still & know that I AM GOD

KEY WORDS	DEFINITIONS	CROSS REFERENCES

MAIN POINT(S)

APPLY

PRAY

Mirror
2 Cor 3:18

day *five*

EPHESIANS 1 | REVIEW & DISCUSSION QUESTIONS

In the fire
~~Read the child of God~~
Calls us & blessing.

1 Summary:	2 Write out a favorite verse(s) from the passage, perhaps in your own words: *for* *Christ rules above all powers on Earth and above all names not only now, but in the future*
3 Why do you think Paul refers to the Ephesians as saints (1:1)? What defines saints? Can you apply this term to yourself? *We believe led by spirit Bold —*	4 In what ways do the blessings of the Father overflow "in Christ" (1:4-14)? *Remember to record these in the table on page 33.*
5 Re-read the list. Which ones touch your heart? Why? *Blameless* *Bold* *Faithful* *Steadful* *Humble* *Meek*	6 Redemption (1:7) is not a commonly used word today. What does Paul mean?

7 What is our promised inheritance? How can we know we will receive this (1:11-14)?

8 Remembering these many blessings leads Paul to do what (1:16)? What characterizes Paul's prayer?

9 What specific things does Paul pray for concerning the Ephesians?

G with hand

10 What do you learn about prayer and praying for others from Paul's example?

11 In your day-to-day life, what does the reality of being "in Christ" mean to you personally? What diverts your focus from God's blessings?

12 Praise God for at least one truth from this week's study:

take it to *heart*

USE THIS SPACE TO WRITE OUT OR JOURNAL A FAVORITE
VERSE OR PASSAGE FROM THIS WEEK'S STUDY

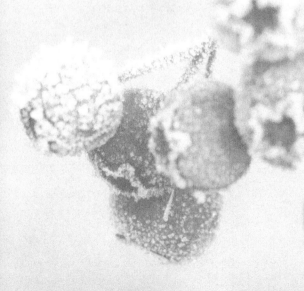

IN LOVE HE PREDESTINED
US FOR ADOPTION TO
HIMSELF AS SONS...

EPHESIANS 1:4-5

chapter *two*

EPHESIANS

take *note*

NOTES ON EPHESIANS 2

take *note*

NOTES ON EPHESIANS 2

day *one*

READ	OBSERVE	INTERPRET
[1] And you were dead in the trespasses and sins [2] in which you once walked, following the course of this world, following the prince of the power of the air, the spirit that is now at work in the sons of disobedience— [3] among whom we all once lived in the passions of our flesh, carrying out the desires of the body and the mind, and were by nature children of wrath, like the rest of mankind. [4] But God, being rich in mercy, because of the great love with which he loved us, [5] even when we were dead in our trespasses, made us alive together with Christ—by grace you have been saved— [6] and raised us up with him and seated us with him in the heavenly places in Christ Jesus, [7] so that in the coming ages he might show the immeasurable riches of his grace in kindness toward us in Christ Jesus.		

KEY WORDS	DEFINITIONS	CROSS REFERENCES

MAIN POINT(S)

But God

APPLY

PRAY

day *two*

EPHESIANS 2:8-10

READ	OBSERVE	INTERPRET
[8] For by grace you have been saved through faith. And this is not your own doing; it is the gift of God, [9] not a result of works, so that no one may boast. [10] For we are his workmanship, created in Christ Jesus for good works, which God prepared beforehand, that we should walk in them.		

KEY WORDS	DEFINITIONS	CROSS REFERENCES
boast workmanship created prepared beforehand .		

MAIN POINT(S)

APPLY

PRAY

day *three*

READ	OBSERVE	INTERPRET
[11] Therefore remember that at one time you Gentiles in the flesh, called "the uncircumcision" by what is called the circumcision, which is made in the flesh by hands— [12] remember that you were at that time separated from Christ, alienated from the commonwealth of Israel and strangers to the covenants of promise, having no hope and without God in the world. [13] But now in Christ Jesus you who once were far off have been brought near by the blood of Christ. [14] For he himself is our peace, who has made us both one and has broken down in his flesh the dividing wall of hostility [15] by abolishing the law of commandments expressed in ordinances, that he might create in himself one new man in place of the two, so making peace, [16] and might reconcile us both to God in one body through the cross, thereby killing the hostility. [17] And he came and preached peace to you who were far off and peace to those who were near.		

KEY WORDS	DEFINITIONS	CROSS REFERENCES
circumcision *abolishing*		

MAIN POINT(S)	APPLY

PRAY

day *four*

EPHESIANS 2:18-22

READ	OBSERVE	INTERPRET
[18] For through him we both have access in one Spirit to the Father. [19] So then you are no longer strangers and aliens, but you are fellow citizens with the saints and members of the household of God, [20] built on the foundation of the apostles and prophets, Christ Jesus himself being the cornerstone, [21] in whom the whole structure, being joined together, grows into a holy temple in the Lord. [22] In him you also are being built together into a dwelling place for God by the Spirit.		

KEY WORDS	DEFINITIONS	CROSS REFERENCES
citizens		

MAIN POINT(S)	APPLY

PRAY

day *five*

EPHESIANS 2 | REVIEW & DISCUSSION QUESTIONS

1 Summary:	2 Write out a favorite verse(s) from the passage, perhaps in your own words: 2:14-17 is DEAD!
3 What does Paul mean by "you were dead in your trespasses and sins" (2:1)? Not alive sin = death	4 Describe Paul's portrayal of walking "dead in sin" (2:2-3). Do you remember what this looked like in your own life? Doing what I felt like doing.
5 Explain the phrase "by grace you have been saved." Not by anything I have done. I deserve death. His Grace comes from His Love for us.	6 What did saving grace look like in your own life? How does your life look different today because of grace?

7 What does it mean to be "God's workmanship?" How might this idea personally encourage you today?

Fearfully & Wonderfully made by God.
He gave us gifts,
talents, freckles,
crooked toes & all.

8 What does Paul want the Ephesians to "remember" (2:11)?

Remember our old life
How we were seperated
from Christ

9 Explain why Gentiles were alienated from the "commonwealth of Israel" (2:12). How do these two groups become one (2:13-16)?

circumscision

thru the CROSS

10 List the three word pictures that Paul uses to describe the unity of the church in Christ (2:15-16, 2:19, and 2:20-22). Choose your favorite one and explain why.

(1) one new man, in place of (2)
both in one body
Not strangers/aliens → fellow citizens
Foundation w/ Jesus the corner
→ grows into a Temple stone.
Holy

11 Define the peace that Christ preached (2:17). How does Paul's idea of peace differ from how you normally think of peace?

Killing the hostility
between Jews &
Gentiles
Abolished the law

12 Praise God for at least one truth from this week's study:

God will never
leave or
forsake me

take it to *heart*

USE THIS SPACE TO WRITE OUT OR JOURNAL A FAVORITE VERSE OR PASSAGE FROM THIS WEEK'S STUDY

FOR HE HIMSELF

IS OUR PEACE...

EPHESIANS 2:14

chapter *three*

EPHESIANS

take *note*

NOTES ON EPHESIANS 3

take *note*

NOTES ON EPHESIANS 3

day *one*

READ	OBSERVE	INTERPRET
[1] For this reason I, Paul, a prisoner of Christ Jesus on behalf of you Gentiles— [2] assuming that you have heard of the stewardship of God's grace that was given to me for you, [3] how the mystery was made known to me by revelation, as I have written briefly. [4] When you read this, you can perceive my insight into the mystery of Christ, [5] which was not made known to the sons of men in other generations as it has now been revealed to his holy apostles and prophets by the Spirit. [6] This mystery is that the Gentiles are fellow heirs, members of the same body, and partakers of the promise in Christ Jesus through the gospel.		

KEY WORDS	DEFINITIONS	CROSS REFERENCES

MAIN POINT(S)

APPLY

PRAY

day *two*

EPHESIANS 3:7-13

READ	OBSERVE	INTERPRET
7 Of this gospel I was made a minister according to the gift of God's grace, which was given me by the working of his power. 8 To me, though I am the very least of all the saints, this grace was given, to preach to the Gentiles the unsearchable riches of Christ, 9 and to bring to light for everyone what is the plan of the mystery hidden for ages in God, who created all things, 10 so that through the church the manifold wisdom of God might now be made known to the rulers and authorities in the heavenly places. 11 This was according to the eternal purpose that he has realized in Christ Jesus our Lord, 12 in whom we have boldness and access with confidence through our faith in him. 13 So I ask you not to lose heart over what I am suffering for you, which is your glory.		

KEY WORDS	DEFINITIONS	CROSS REFERENCES

MAIN POINT(S)	APPLY

PRAY

day *three*

EPHESIANS 3:14-19

READ	OBSERVE
For today's reading, please look up the passage in your own Bible and hand-write the verses here.	
	INTERPRET

KEY WORDS	DEFINITIONS	CROSS REFERENCES

MAIN POINT(S)

APPLY

PRAY

day *four*

EPHESIANS 3:20-21

READ	OBSERVE	INTERPRET
²⁰ Now to him who is able to do far more abundantly than all that we ask or think, according to the power at work within us, ²¹ to him be glory in the church and in Christ Jesus throughout all generations, forever and ever. Amen.		

KEY WORDS	DEFINITIONS	CROSS REFERENCES

MAIN POINT(S)

APPLY

PRAY

day *five*

1 Summary:	2 Write out a favorite verse(s) from the passage, perhaps in your own words:
3 How vested is Paul in the gospel for the sake of the Ephesians (3:1)? How do you know?	4 What mystery is Paul referring to in verses 3 and 4?
5 Why does Paul consider himself the least of the saints (3:8)?	6 How would you describe or explain the "unsearchable riches of Jesus Christ" (3:8) to an unbeliever?

7 Practically, in our day-to-day life, in what ways can we, like Paul, remember how "rich" we are in Christ?

8 In verse 14, Paul states that "I bow my knee before the Father." For what purpose and what do you learn through Paul's example?

9 What are Paul's specific prayer requests on behalf of the Ephesians (3:14-21)?

10 Which request most touches your heart? Why?

11 Take a moment to marvel at God's power. In what ways does His power differ from your own power? In what ways are you tapping into His power?

12 Praise God for at least one truth from this week's study:

take it to *heart*

USE THIS SPACE TO WRITE OUT OR JOURNAL A FAVORITE
VERSE OR PASSAGE FROM THIS WEEK'S STUDY

...THAT YOU, BEING
ROOTED AND GROUNDED
IN LOVE, MAY... KNOW
THE LOVE OF CHRIST THAT
SURPASSES KNOWLEDGE...

EPHESIANS 3:17-19

chapter *four*

EPHESIANS

take *note*

NOTES ON EPHESIANS 4

take *note*

NOTES ON EPHESIANS 4

day *one*

EPHESIANS 4:1-6

READ	OBSERVE	INTERPRET
[1] I therefore, a prisoner for the Lord, urge you to walk in a manner worthy of the calling to which you have been called, [2] with all humility and gentleness, with patience, bearing with one another in love, [3] eager to maintain the unity of the Spirit in the bond of peace. [4] There is one body and one Spirit—just as you were called to the one hope that belongs to your call— [5] one Lord, one faith, one baptism, [6] one God and Father of all, who is over all and through all and in all.		

KEY WORDS	DEFINITIONS	CROSS REFERENCES

MAIN POINT(S)

APPLY

PRAY

day *two*

EPHESIANS 4:7-16

READ	OBSERVE	INTERPRET
⁷ But grace was given to each one of us according to the measure of Christ's gift. ⁸ Therefore it says, "When he ascended on high he led a host of captives, and he gave gifts to men." ⁹ (In saying, "He ascended," what does it mean but that he had also descended into the lower regions, the earth? ¹⁰ He who descended is the one who also ascended far above all the heavens, that he might fill all things.) ¹¹ And he gave the apostles, the prophets, the evangelists, the shepherds and teachers, ¹² to equip the saints for the work of ministry, for building up the body of Christ, ¹³ until we all attain to the unity of the faith and of the knowledge of the Son of God, to mature manhood, to the measure of the stature of the fullness of Christ, ¹⁴ so that we may no longer be children, tossed to and fro by the waves and carried about by every wind of doctrine, by human cunning, by craftiness in deceitful schemes. ¹⁵ Rather, speaking the truth in love, we are to grow up in every way into him who is the head, into Christ, ¹⁶ from whom the whole body, joined and held together by every joint with which it is equipped, when each part is working properly, makes the body grow so that it builds itself up in love.		

KEY WORDS	DEFINITIONS	CROSS REFERENCES

MAIN POINT(S)

APPLY

PRAY

day *three*

EPHESIANS 4:17-24

READ	OBSERVE	INTERPRET
[17] Now this I say and testify in the Lord, that you must no longer walk as the Gentiles do, in the futility of their minds. [18] They are darkened in their understanding, alienated from the life of God because of the ignorance that is in them, due to their hardness of heart. [19] They have become callous and have given themselves up to sensuality, greedy to practice every kind of impurity. [20] But that is not the way you learned Christ!— [21] assuming that you have heard about him and were taught in him, as the truth is in Jesus, [22] to put off your old self, which belongs to your former manner of life and is corrupt through deceitful desires, [23] and to be renewed in the spirit of your minds, [24] and to put on the new self, created after the likeness of God in true righteousness and holiness.		

KEY WORDS	DEFINITIONS	CROSS REFERENCES

MAIN POINT(S)

APPLY

PRAY

day *four*

EPHESIANS 4:25-32

READ	OBSERVE	INTERPRET
25 Therefore, having put away falsehood, let each one of you speak the truth with his neighbor, for we are members one of another. 26 Be angry and do not sin; do not let the sun go down on your anger, 27 and give no opportunity to the devil. 28 Let the thief no longer steal, but rather let him labor, doing honest work with his own hands, so that he may have something to share with anyone in need. 29 Let no corrupting talk come out of your mouths, but only such as is good for building up, as fits the occasion, that it may give grace to those who hear. 30 And do not grieve the Holy Spirit of God, by whom you were sealed for the day of redemption. 31 Let all bitterness and wrath and anger and clamor and slander be put away from you, along with all malice. 32 Be kind to one another, tenderhearted, forgiving one another, as God in Christ forgave you.		

KEY WORDS	DEFINITIONS	CROSS REFERENCES

MAIN POINT(S)

APPLY

PRAY

day *five*

1 Summary:	2 Write out a favorite verse(s) from the passage, perhaps in your own words:
3 "Therefore" is a transition word. What transition does Paul make in verse 1?	4 What does it mean "to walk?" How are we to walk (4:2-3)? If you could have an extra helping of one of these character traits, which would it be? Explain.
5 How do we have unity with other believers throughout the world (4:4-6)?	6 According to Paul, what characterizes a mature Christian (4:11-15)? How are you helping to mature others?

7 How do thinking and behavior go hand in hand (4:17-18)?

8 Describe the ways of the "old self" (4:17-22). Which one do you need to "put off?" What step can you take today? Practically speaking, how do we "put off" the old self and "put on" the new self?

9 In verses 25-32, Paul lays out specific ways to walk worthy of our calling. List these.

10 Which of these directives touches or convicts your heart today? Why? Talk to God about it.

11 What does Paul mean when he says, "do not grieve the Holy Spirit" (4:30)?

12 Praise God for at least one truth from this week's study:

take it to *heart*

USE THIS SPACE TO WRITE OUT OR JOURNAL A FAVORITE
VERSE OR PASSAGE FROM THIS WEEK'S STUDY

PUT ON THE NEW SELF,
CREATED AFTER THE
LIKENESS OF GOD IN
TRUE RIGHTEOUSNESS
AND HOLINESS.

EPHESIANS 4:24

chapter *five*

EPHESIANS

take *note*

NOTES ON EPHESIANS 5

take *note*

NOTES ON EPHESIANS 5

day *one*

EPHESIANS 5:1-6

READ	OBSERVE	INTERPRET
[1] Therefore be imitators of God, as beloved children. [2] And walk in love, as Christ loved us and gave himself up for us, a fragrant offering and sacrifice to God. [3] But sexual immorality and all impurity or covetousness must not even be named among you, as is proper among saints. [4] Let there be no filthiness nor foolish talk nor crude joking, which are out of place, but instead let there be thanksgiving. [5] For you may be sure of this, that everyone who is sexually immoral or impure, or who is covetous (that is, an idolater), has no inheritance in the kingdom of Christ and God. [6] Let no one deceive you with empty words, for because of these things the wrath of God comes upon the sons of disobedience.		

KEY WORDS	DEFINITIONS	CROSS REFERENCES

MAIN POINT(S)	APPLY

PRAY

day *two*

EPHESIANS 5:7-14

READ	OBSERVE	INTERPRET
[7] Therefore do not become partners with them; [8] for at one time you were darkness, but now you are light in the Lord. Walk as children of light [9] (for the fruit of light is found in all that is good and right and true), [10] and try to discern what is pleasing to the Lord. [11] Take no part in the unfruitful works of darkness, but instead expose them. [12] For it is shameful even to speak of the things that they do in secret. [13] But when anything is exposed by the light, it becomes visible, [14] for anything that becomes visible is light. Therefore it says, "Awake, O sleeper, and arise from the dead, and Christ will shine on you."		

KEY WORDS	DEFINITIONS	CROSS REFERENCES

MAIN POINT(S)

APPLY

PRAY

day *three*

EPHESIANS 5:15-21

READ	OBSERVE	INTERPRET
[15] Look carefully then how you walk, not as unwise but as wise, [16] making the best use of the time, because the days are evil. [17] Therefore do not be foolish, but understand what the will of the Lord is. [18] And do not get drunk with wine, for that is debauchery, but be filled with the Spirit, [19] addressing one another in psalms and hymns and spiritual songs, singing and making melody to the Lord with your heart, [20] giving thanks always and for everything to God the Father in the name of our Lord Jesus Christ, [21] submitting to one another out of reverence for Christ.		

KEY WORDS	DEFINITIONS	CROSS REFERENCES

MAIN POINT(S)

APPLY

PRAY

day *four*

READ	OBSERVE	INTERPRET
22 Wives, submit to your own husbands, as to the Lord. 23 For the husband is the head of the wife even as Christ is the head of the church, his body, and is himself its Savior. 24 Now as the church submits to Christ, so also wives should submit in everything to their husbands. 25 Husbands, love your wives, as Christ loved the church and gave himself up for her, 26 that he might sanctify her, having cleansed her by the washing of water with the word, 27 so that he might present the church to himself in splendor, without spot or wrinkle or any such thing, that she might be holy and without blemish. 28 In the same way husbands should love their wives as their own bodies. He who loves his wife loves himself. 29 For no one ever hated his own flesh, but nourishes and cherishes it, just as Christ does the church, 30 because we are members of his body. 31 "Therefore a man shall leave his father and mother and hold fast to his wife, and the two shall become one flesh." 32 This mystery is profound, and I am saying that it refers to Christ and the church. 33 However, let each one of you love his wife as himself, and let the wife see that she respects her husband.		

KEY WORDS	DEFINITIONS	CROSS REFERENCES

MAIN POINT(S)

APPLY

PRAY

day *five*

EPHESIANS 5 | REVIEW & DISCUSSION QUESTIONS

1 Summary:	2 Write out a favorite verse(s) from the passage, perhaps in your own words:
3 How do we imitate God (5:1-2)?	4 According to verses 3-9, what offenses characterize a person of darkness? Which ones present a personal struggle to you?
5 What characterizes a person of the light (5:9)?	6 List the basic commands Paul gives children of the light in verses 4-21.

7 How do we "discern what is pleasing to the Lord" and "understand what the will of the Lord is" (5:17)?

8 Why does Paul command believers to "be filled with the Spirit" (5:17)?

9 How are songs and hymns important to you?

10 What instruction does God give to wives? What instruction does God give to husbands?

11 How can understanding your position "in Christ" help you manage specific relationship issues you face today?

12 Praise God for at least one truth from this week's study:

take it to *heart*

USE THIS SPACE TO WRITE OUT OR JOURNAL A FAVORITE
VERSE OR PASSAGE FROM THIS WEEK'S STUDY

AND WALK IN LOVE, AS
CHRIST LOVED US AND GAVE
HIMSELF UP FOR US...

EPHESIANS 5:2

chapter *six*

EPHESIANS

take *note*

NOTES ON EPHESIANS 6

take *note*

NOTES ON EPHESIANS 6

day *one*

EPHESIANS 6:1-4

READ	OBSERVE	INTERPRET
[1] Children, obey your parents in the Lord, for this is right. [2] "Honor your father and mother" (this is the first commandment with a promise), [3] "that it may go well with you and that you may live long in the land." [4] Fathers, do not provoke your children to anger, but bring them up in the discipline and instruction of the Lord.		

KEY WORDS	DEFINITIONS	CROSS REFERENCES

MAIN POINT(S)

APPLY

PRAY

day *two*

EPHESIANS 6:5-9

READ	OBSERVE	INTERPRET
[5] Bondservants, obey your earthly masters with fear and trembling, with a sincere heart, as you would Christ, [6] not by the way of eye-service, as people-pleasers, but as bondservants of Christ, doing the will of God from the heart, [7] rendering service with a good will as to the Lord and not to man, [8] knowing that whatever good anyone does, this he will receive back from the Lord, whether he is a bond-servant or is free. [9] Masters, do the same to them, and stop your threatening, knowing that he who is both their Master and yours is in heaven, and that there is no partiality with him.		

KEY WORDS	DEFINITIONS	CROSS REFERENCES

MAIN POINT(S)

APPLY

PRAY

day *three*

EPHESIANS 6:10-20

READ	OBSERVE	INTERPRET
[10] Finally, be strong in the Lord and in the strength of his might. [11] Put on the whole armor of God, that you may be able to stand against the schemes of the devil. [12] For we do not wrestle against flesh and blood, but against the rulers, against the authorities, against the cosmic powers over this present darkness, against the spiritual forces of evil in the heavenly places. [13] Therefore take up the whole armor of God, that you may be able to withstand in the evil day, and having done all, to stand firm. [14] Stand therefore, having fastened on the belt of truth, and having put on the breastplate of righteousness, [15] and, as shoes for your feet, having put on the readiness given by the gospel of peace. [16] In all circumstances take up the shield of faith, with which you can extinguish all the flaming darts of the evil one; [17] and take the helmet of salvation, and the sword of the Spirit, which is the word of God, [18] praying at all times in the Spirit, with all prayer and supplication. To that end, keep alert with all perseverance, making supplication for all the saints, [19] and also for me, that words may be given to me in opening my mouth boldly to proclaim the mystery of the gospel, [20] for which I am an ambassador in chains, that I may declare it boldly, as I ought to speak.		

KEY WORDS	DEFINITIONS	CROSS REFERENCES

MAIN POINT(S)

APPLY

PRAY

day *four*

EPHESIANS 6:21-24

READ	OBSERVE	INTERPRET
[21] So that you also may know how I am and what I am doing, Tychicus the beloved brother and faithful minister in the Lord will tell you everything. [22] I have sent him to you for this very purpose, that you may know how we are, and that he may encourage your hearts. [23] Peace be to the brothers, and love with faith, from God the Father and the Lord Jesus Christ. [24] Grace be with all who love our Lord Jesus Christ with love incorruptible.		

KEY WORDS	DEFINITIONS	CROSS REFERENCES

MAIN POINT(S)

APPLY

PRAY

day *five*

EPHESIANS 6 | REVIEW & DISCUSSION QUESTIONS

1 Summary:	2 Write out a favorite verse(s) from the passage, perhaps in your own words:
3 In your own words, what does it mean for children to "honor your father and mother?" How do you live out this command today (6:1-3)?	4 Paul also gives clear instruction to parents. What does this look like in everyday life?
5 During the first century, the slave/master relationship was a common employer/employee relationship. What do you learn about work relationships from verses 5-9?	6 Beginning in verse 10, Paul seeks to arouse believers to action. Describe.

7 What are the six pieces that make up the armor of God?

8 Choose one piece of God's armor to better understand. Explain its purpose.

9 How do you normally handle spiritual battles? How does it compare to Paul's suggestion?

10 What specific instructions does Paul give for prayer (6:18-19)?

11 In making a personal prayer request, Paul could have asked for any given number of things. What does he ask? Share your thoughts about this.

12 Praise God for at least one truth from this week's study:

take it to *heart*

USE THIS SPACE TO WRITE OUT OR JOURNAL A FAVORITE
VERSE OR PASSAGE FROM THIS WEEK'S STUDY

FINALLY, BE STRONG IN
THE LORD AND IN THE
STRENGTH OF HIS MIGHT.

EPHESIANS 6:10

final *thoughts*

WRAPPING UP

final *thoughts*

THE BOOK OF EPHESIANS | WRAPPING UP

1 Choose your favorite verse from Ephesians. Write it out here. Give an explanation of what this verse means to you or why you find it impactful.	2 Consider the book of Ephesians as a whole. What overarching themes did you notice within this book throughout your study?
3 How would you summarize the book of Ephesians in a single word?	4 Praise God for a truth that He has revealed to you or for a way that He has worked in your life as a result of your study of Ephesians:

pause and *reflect*

USE THIS SPACE TO WRITE OUT A PRAYER, A KEY PASSAGE, OR A REFLECTION ON YOUR STUDY OF EPHESIANS

...YOU WHO ONCE WERE
FAR OFF HAVE BEEN
BROUGHT NEAR BY
THE BLOOD OF CHRIST.

EPHESIANS 2:13

leader *guide*

MAXIMIZING THE SMALL-GROUP EXPERIENCE

GO THEREFORE AND MAKE
DISCIPLES OF ALL NATIONS,
BAPTIZING THEM IN THE
NAME OF THE FATHER AND
OF THE SON AND OF THE
HOLY SPIRIT, TEACHING THEM
TO OBSERVE ALL THAT I
HAVE COMMANDED YOU.

MATTHEW 28:19-20

introduction
LEADING WOMEN THROUGH **SIMPLY BIBLE**

Welcome to **SIMPLY BIBLE,** and thank you for your commitment to walk alongside a group of women for this season of exploring God's Word. In my own life, God has proven Himself faithful. Time and again as I lead women and seek to be a blessing to others, the blessing always seems to be mine. He is gracious that way. So, it is my heartfelt prayer for leaders that, as you seek to be a blessing to others, you too will be blessed beyond measure by the experience of shepherding women through God's Word. Truly, what a privilege it is to facilitate conversations that point women to Christ!

The primary objective of **SIMPLY BIBLE** is this:

> To inspire every woman to love God with all her heart, soul, mind, and strength, and to love others as herself. (Luke 10:27)

And *you*, the small-group leader, will play an important role in inspiring women to do exactly that! You will lead your group through meaningful conversations, with the help of the discussion questions found at the end of every chapter in this workbook. Our intention here is to help women grow in their relationships with Jesus Christ. It is also my hope that you will connect with the women in your groups on a personal level, gently guiding them to authentic relationships with one another.

guarding your *heart*

LEADING FROM THE RIGHT PERSPECTIVE

Ethos is a Latin word that denotes the fundamental character or spirit of a community, group, or person. When used to discuss dramatic literature, ethos is that moral element used to determine a character's action rather than his or her thought or emotion. Ethos points to the inward being, to the moral fabric of the heart. In Biblical language, ethos absolutely compares to a person's heart. And our ethos, our heart, is important to God.

His Word tells us:

> Above all else, guard your heart,
> for everything you do flows from it.
> *Proverbs 4:23 NIV*

Above all else, guard your heart. Why? Because everything we do flows from the heart, from our inward being. And that "everything" includes leading women through God's Word. If we want to see women growing in authentic relationships with Christ and with one another, that process must first begin in our own hearts.

> For the Lord sees not as man sees: man looks on the
> outward appearance, but the Lord looks on the heart.
> *I Samuel 16:7*

So often, as individuals and as women's ministry groups, we get caught up in appearances. I'm guilty. How easy it is for us as leaders to dress ourselves up for Bible study, look nice on the outside, make sure the tables are inviting, share a few pleasant words, all the while never touching the core or the heart in order to make heart connections with God and with one another. God looks at the heart. Perhaps we should, too.

Truly, I believe that I could write a book concerning effectively "guarding our hearts" while leading women in inductive Bible study. However, for our purposes today, let's keep things simple and limit our necessary ingredients to three:

(1) Jesus
(2) Prayer
(3) The Word

By guarding our hearts in these ways, successful Bible study leadership is certain. Let's briefly understand.

GUARDING YOUR HEART WITH **JESUS**

This may seem so obvious, but honestly, isn't it easy for us to miss the forest for the trees? How can we expect our ladies to believe if we ourselves are not believing Jesus and His Word? Without Jesus and His Word dwelling in our hearts, we're not going to overflow with Him and His Spirit. Our efforts will certainly ring hollow. Paul puts it this way:

> If I speak in the tongues of men and of angels, but
> have not love, I am a noisy gong or a clanging cymbal.
> *I Corinthians 13:1*

None of us wants to annoy others as a gong gone wrong. But without a personal heart connection to His heart of love, we labor in our own strength. One of my leaders referred to this kind of fruit as being like the "fake grapes" found in her Grandma's kitchen. Rather, we are after the juicy sweet fruit of the Spirit that comes from abiding in the True Vine. To overflow with Christ, one must first abide in Him:

> Abide in me, and I in you. As the branch cannot
> bear fruit by itself, unless it abides in the vine,
> neither can you, unless you abide in me.
> *John 15:4*

Abiding in Jesus is the secret, powerful ingredient to leading Bible study. Okay, maybe it's not so secret, but it is powerful! Some days we feel that heart connection with God and other days we do not, but we can know we are abiding when we are obeying and seeking to follow His will.

Are you daily abiding with The Word from the inside out? Our character and our inner lives ought to align with our outward appearance. There is nothing more effective than a woman leading others with a sanctified and authentic heart. This transformation happens as a woman applies Scripture, yields to God's will and allows for the Spirit's holy work to happen within her own heart. That leads to true beauty. It's attractive. Others will want to follow. Peter says it this way:

> Let your adorning be the hidden person of the heart
> with the imperishable beauty of a gentle and quiet spirit,
> which in God's sight is very precious.
> *I Peter 3:4*

GUARDING YOUR HEART WITH **PRAYER**

Here, again, the need for prayer is likely obvious, but sometimes when we get caught up in the details, we overlook the obvious. Pray, pray, and pray! If Jesus required prayer in order to remain united with the Father in both purpose and mission, surely we need it more. Prayer helps us to stay focused on Christ, the Good Shepherd who leads the way to green pastures. As we study His Word, we desire to follow Christ to these places that teem with His life and living water. However, without Christ to do the heavy lifting of paving the way and clearing the path, we will struggle to get there. And so, we pray.

Set aside time to pray for Bible study. If your schedule allows, before you begin leading this study, take one day away from other activities to commit the weeks ahead to Him.

Remember that prayer is simply sharing your heart and relating with God. It involves both speaking and listening. I find the acronym *P.R.A.Y.* to be useful, especially when praying in groups. This template allows groups to walk through four steps of prayer:

P	PRAISE	Acknowledge your dependence on Him; yield to His ways.

> Blessed are those who have learned to acclaim you,
> who walk in the light of your presence, Lord.
> *Psalm 89:15 NIV*

Beginning a session with praise turns our hearts toward God. In a group setting, I find it effective to encourage short "popcorn prayers" of praise where women take turns utilizing simple words and phrases to worship God. For example:

- I praise You, God, as the Light of the world.
- I praise You for You are mighty to save.
- Lord, You are Life.
- You are the truth.

R	REPENT	Confess and agree with God concerning sin.

> If we confess our sins, he is faithful and just to forgive
> us our sins and to cleanse us from all unrighteousness.
> *I John 1:9*

Offer group members a silent moment to allow for private confession.

A	ADORE	Admire and thank God for His ways.

> Let us come into his presence with thanksgiving;
> let us make a joyful noise to him with songs of praise!
> *Psalm 95:2*

Thanksgiving is a beautiful way to end a Bible study session. Together, give thanks to the Lord for all that He has revealed.

Y	YIELD	Acknowledge your dependence on God. Yield to His ways.

> Whoever abides in me and I in him, he it is that bears much
> fruit, for apart from me you can do nothing. | *John 15:5*
>
> Delight yourself in the Lord, and he will give you the
> desires of your heart. | *Psalm 37:4*

With that, what sorts of things shall we *yield* to God? Here are a few ideas and ways to align with God's heart:

- May God be glorified through the study.
- May God's Will be accomplished in the hearts of women.
- May women know, believe, and abide in Christ.
- May women's hearts be united with His and with one another.
- May God offer protection from all distractions as women commit to studying God's Word.
- May God's Word transform hearts and lives, that women would be holy as He is holy.

GUARDING YOUR HEART WITH **THE WORD**
Read. Reflect. Remember His Word.

Whether teaching a large group or facilitating discussion in a small group, it's easy for leaders to fall into the trap of thinking that we need to have all of the right answers. Furthermore, we often feel the need to be able to speak all those answers eloquently. Due to this false thinking, many leaders spend countless hours scouring commentaries. And we wear ourselves out! After all, God's Word is so deep and rich that we will not plumb the depths of a Scripture passage in just one week. Thinking we need to have all the right answers is a fallacy.

Yes! Without a doubt, commentaries have their valuable place for solid interpretation. (Interpretation is that portion of inductive study where women should all be on the same page.) However, the risk to leaders who spend too much time delving into their commentaries is that the workbook journals plus the teaching and discussion times will reflect the commentaries versus the scripture itself.

To counter this, we simply need time in God's Word. As we read, observe and marinate in the Bible text itself, God's Spirit teaches and leads. His Word speaks on its own. It's powerful and effective. We can trust in it!

So shall my word be that goes out from my mouth;
it shall not return to me empty, but it shall
accomplish that which I purpose, and
shall succeed in the thing for which I sent it.
Isaiah 55:11

Read, read, and read again. Read the daily Scripture passage using various translations. Read aloud, and read slowly. Ponder. Listen to the Word while driving. Talk about what you are learning and discovering in the Word with family and friends. This will help you be prepared to speak it when time for Bible study. Just as we marinate meat to soften, tenderize, and flavor it, we "sit in" the text allowing God's Spirit to soften, tenderize and flavor our hearts and minds with His personal message.

I have stored up your word in my heart,
that I might not sin against you.
Psalm 119:11

A challenging but brilliant way to soak in Scripture is memorization. Memorization is hard work, but the payoff is great. Scripture becomes embedded within us and can overflow from the heart when needed. Certainly, those Scriptures guard my own heart. And in leading, I have noticed that reciting Scripture over women deeply touches their hearts in a way that nothing else does.

Ideally, when studying in groups, teachers and small group leaders should prepare the study a week ahead of time. Yep! You read that right. Seek to be one week ahead of the regular study schedule. Then, allow time for leaders to review together before leading and teaching in groups the following week. The benefits of discussing, sharing, and grappling with the Word as leaders are priceless for preparation and confidence in leading. Also, through that time, God will knit together the hearts of the leaders. That dynamic will then transform the ethos or heart of the group as a whole.

Guarding hearts with Jesus, prayer, and His Word prepares us for life-changing and dynamic conversations around our Bible study tables. In fact, by communing with Jesus and His Spirit through prayer and His Word, you truly have all you need in order to successfully lead a group.

> But you will receive power when the Holy Spirit
> has come upon you, and you will be my witnesses
> in Jerusalem and in all Judea and Samaria,
> and to the end of the earth.
> *Acts 1:8*

The following tools and resources included in this appendix may provide additional help and support as you endeavor to lead your group. Use them however you find them to be helpful.

- Effective Leadership Guide
- Weekly Preparation Guide
- Bible Study Schedule
- Small Group Roster
- Attendance Record
- Prayer Log

effective *leadership*

A GUIDE TO LEADING A SMALL GROUP EFFECTIVELY

Remember that the goal for our study is to see women growing in relationship with Christ and one another. You do not need to be a Bible expert to lead women in discussion about His Word. You only need a heart to love and encourage women. So, what does effective small group leadership look like?

ENCOURAGING | In an *encouraging* small group, all participants feel included and welcome to share freely. Thoughts and ideas are respected, and women are cheered on in their efforts to grow closer to God through their study of His Word.

BIBLICALLY SOUND | When we endeavor to create a *biblically-sound* environment, we point women in the direction of truth and correct doctrine, gently guiding them away from wrong thinking.

BALANCED | In a group that is *balanced,* shy or quiet women are drawn out and encouraged to participate in discussions, while "over-sharers" are encouraged to listen to others and not to dominate the conversation.

WISE | A *wise* small group leader recognizes when the conversation is getting off-topic or veering toward gossip. In such situations, it is a good idea to redirect women back to the ultimate focus of the meeting: God's Word.

PRAYERFUL | A *prayerful* group leader is an asset to her group. She prays regularly for her group members and facilitates opportunities for them to pray for one another.

CONFIDENTIAL | Group members should feel secure that the things they share will remain *confidential.* An effective small group leader is committed to preserving the privacy of her group members.

I AM THE VINE; YOU
ARE THE BRANCHES.
WHOEVER ABIDES IN ME
AND I IN HIM, HE IT IS
THAT BEARS MUCH FRUIT,
FOR APART FROM ME
YOU CAN DO NOTHING.

JOHN 15:5

weekly preparation guide

PREPARING FOR SMALL-GROUP MEETINGS

WEEK ONE | EPHESIANS 1

- [ ] Read the assigned daily passages.
- [ ] Use each daily framework to observe, interpret, and apply.
- [ ] Respond to all of the Day 5 questions.
- [ ] Pray for your small group meeting and for your group members.

1 What does this week's study tell me about God?	2 What does this week's study tell me about how I am to relate to Him?

WEEK TWO | EPHESIANS 2

- [ ] Read the assigned daily passages.
- [ ] Use each daily framework to observe, interpret, and apply.
- [ ] Respond to all of the Day 5 questions.
- [ ] Pray for your small group meeting and for your group members.

1 What does this week's study tell me about God?	2 What does this week's study tell me about how I am to relate to Him?

WEEK THREE | EPHESIANS 3

☐   Read the assigned daily passages.

☐   Use each daily framework to observe, interpret, and apply.

☐   Respond to all of the Day 5 questions.

☐   Pray for your small group meeting and for your group members.

1 What does this week's study tell me about God?	2 What does this week's study tell me about how I am to relate to Him?

WEEK FOUR | EPHESIANS 4

☐   Read the assigned daily passages.

☐   Use each daily framework to observe, interpret, and apply.

☐   Respond to all of the Day 5 questions.

☐   Pray for your small group meeting and for your group members.

1 What does this week's study tell me about God?	2 What does this week's study tell me about how I am to relate to Him?

WEEK FIVE | EPHESIANS 5

☐ Read the assigned daily passages.

☐ Use each daily framework to observe, interpret, and apply.

☐ Respond to all of the Day 5 questions.

☐ Pray for your small group meeting and for your group members.

1 What does this week's study tell me about God?	2 What does this week's study tell me about how I am to relate to Him?

WEEK SIX | EPHESIANS 6

☐ Read the assigned daily passages.

☐ Use each daily framework to observe, interpret, and apply.

☐ Respond to all of the Day 5 questions.

☐ Pray for your small group meeting and for your group members.

1 What does this week's study tell me about God?	2 What does this week's study tell me about how I am to relate to Him?

ALL SCRIPTURE IS BREATHED
OUT BY GOD AND PROFITABLE
FOR TEACHING, FOR REPROOF,
FOR CORRECTION, AND FOR
TRAINING IN RIGHTEOUSNESS,
THAT THE MAN OF GOD MAY
BE COMPLETE, EQUIPPED FOR
EVERY GOOD WORK.

2 TIMOTHY 3:16-17

bible study *schedule*

EPHESIANS | A **SIMPLY BIBLE** STUDY

	READING ASSIGNMENT	SMALL GROUP MEETING DATE	LEADER MEETING DATE
WEEK 1			
WEEK 2			
WEEK 3			
WEEK 4			
WEEK 5			
WEEK 6			

small group *roster*

EPHESIANS | A **SIMPLY BIBLE** STUDY

PARTICIPANT LIST

1
2
3
4
5
6
7
8
9
10
11
12
13

NAME	
BIRTHDAY	
PHONE NUMBER	
EMAIL ADDRESS	
CONTACT METHOD	
NOTES	

NAME

BIRTHDAY

PHONE NUMBER

EMAIL ADDRESS

CONTACT METHOD

NOTES

NAME

BIRTHDAY

PHONE NUMBER

EMAIL ADDRESS

CONTACT METHOD

NOTES

NAME

BIRTHDAY

PHONE NUMBER

EMAIL ADDRESS

CONTACT METHOD

NOTES

NAME

BIRTHDAY	
PHONE NUMBER	
EMAIL ADDRESS	
CONTACT METHOD	

NOTES

NAME

BIRTHDAY	
PHONE NUMBER	
EMAIL ADDRESS	
CONTACT METHOD	

NOTES

NAME

BIRTHDAY	
PHONE NUMBER	
EMAIL ADDRESS	
CONTACT METHOD	

NOTES

NAME

BIRTHDAY	
PHONE NUMBER	
EMAIL ADDRESS	
CONTACT METHOD	

NOTES

NAME

BIRTHDAY	
PHONE NUMBER	
EMAIL ADDRESS	
CONTACT METHOD	

NOTES

NAME

BIRTHDAY	
PHONE NUMBER	
EMAIL ADDRESS	
CONTACT METHOD	

NOTES

attendance *log*

EPHESIANS | A **SIMPLY BIBLE** STUDY

PARTICIPANT'S NAME	WEEK 1 | EPHESIANS 1	WEEK 2 | EPHESIANS 2	WEEK 3 | EPHESIANS 3	WEEK 4 | EPHESIANS 4	WEEK 5 | EPHESIANS 5	WEEK 6 | EPHESIANS 6
1						
2						
3						
4						
5						
6						
7						
8						
9						
10						
11						
12						
13						

prayer *log*

EPHESIANS | A **SIMPLY BIBLE** STUDY

DATE	NAME	REQUEST	FOLLOW-UP

DATE	NAME	REQUEST	FOLLOW-UP

DATE	NAME	REQUEST	FOLLOW-UP

DATE	NAME	REQUEST	FOLLOW-UP

DATE	NAME	REQUEST	FOLLOW-UP

AND WE KNOW THAT
FOR THOSE WHO LOVE GOD
ALL THINGS WORK TOGETHER
FOR GOOD, FOR THOSE WHO
ARE CALLED ACCORDING
TO HIS PURPOSE.

ROMANS 8:28

Made in the USA
Middletown, DE
20 September 2023